FROM LAND TO LANDMARK

The hidden science behind perfect home design

FROM LAND TO LANDMARK

The hidden science behind perfect home design

Ar. PIYUSH MITTAL

Worldwide Published by
Pendown Press

PENDOWN PRESS LLP
An ISO 9001 & ISO 14001 Certified Co.,
Regd. Office: 3767A, Kanhaiya Nagar,
Tri Nagar, Delhi-110035
Ph.: 8130886000, 9650072927
E-mail: info@pendownpress.com
Branch Office: 1A/2A, 20, Hari Sadan, Ansari Road,
Daryaganj, New Delhi-110002
Ph.: 011-45794768
Website: PendownPress.com

Edition: 2024
Price: ₹ 299
ISBN: 978-93-6338-477-4

Layout and Cover Designed by Pendown Graphics Team

Dedicated to every plot owner who **dreams of building** not just a house, **but a legacy** –

May your vision find shape, your efforts bear fruit,

And may your home reflect your **finest dreams.**

TABLE OF CONTENTS

PREFACE

Building a home is a beautiful dream, but let me be honest—it can easily turn into a nightmare if you walk in unprepared. Over the years, I've seen people pour their hearts (and wallets) into their dream homes, only to be left disappointed by poor planning, hidden costs, and avoidable mistakes. That's what inspired me to write this book—not as an instruction manual, but as a trusted guide.

This isn't about fancy words or technical theories. It's about real-life insights—things I've learned from hands-on experience. You'll find practical tips on budgeting smartly, selecting materials wisely, and making design decisions that stand the test of time. Most importantly, I'll share the hidden industry secrets that no one talks about—the ones that can save you from costly blunders.

I've kept it simple, straightforward, and easy to follow. Think of it as a friendly conversation over coffee—honest, practical, and to the point. Whether you're building your first home or simply renovating a space, my hope is that this book helps you make smarter choices, avoid unnecessary stress, and enjoy the process.

After all, your home isn't just a structure—it's a reflection of your life, and it deserves nothing less than the best of your decisions.

ACKNOWLEDGEMENTS

Whatever I have achieved in life, would have been impossible without the support of my parents. They've taught me unconditional love and I have seen them grow along with me. The wings that I have today would not have been possible without them.

To my wife Nancy, who has stood by me in every situation. You have handled all family responsibilities with great skill and dedication. Thank you from the bottom of my heart.

To my children, Atharv and Nitaara, who are the source of my happiness and inspiration. Lots of love!

To my team at Next Wall, who have been like partners, mentors, and family. Thank you for walking this journey with me.

My heartfelt gratitude to all my mentors and guides who have shown me light and direction in times of confusion.

To our clients, who have shared their experiences and knowledge with us during this journey—thank you for trusting us and being our inspiration.

A special acknowledgement goes to Dinesh Verma and his exceptional team at Pendown Press. From the initial concept to the final manuscript, their support and expertise have made this book possible.

And finally, to all my loved ones who have been with me on this journey—thank you for your unwavering support, encouragement, and affection. Even if your names are not mentioned, you always hold a special place in my heart.

Without the support of all of you, it would not have been possible for me to move forward with confidence.

INTRODUCTION

Hello, my name is Piyush Mittal. I am a second-generation architect, certified interior designer, and Vastu Acharya specializing in residential design.

My trust in a structured approach to residential plot design and development began early in my career, 16 years ago. Ever since then, it has never failed to impress me—not only in establishing a fearless and frustration-free process for my clients but also in generating referrals through my endless list of happy customers.

I live and breathe the design process daily, and it continues to top my list of step-by-step tasks that deliver measurable results consistently.

Over the years, I have successfully used structured approaches and techniques to build my own award-winning architecture and interior design practice. I have helped numerous clients—industrialists, business owners, traders, professionals, and entrepreneurs—achieve their goal of building an ultra-luxury home without any prior knowledge of construction.

The journey so far has been brilliant!

You must be wondering why I am sharing this book when I could have charged a premium for this secret information. After all, if you implement the suggestions in this book, you can achieve your dream home faster and more efficiently. Besides, as we often learn in business, "there is no free lunch."

So, why am I sharing this sacred information, gathered through 16 years of hands-on experience, in this book?

First, being deeply in love with design and its connected domains, it breaks my heart to see how people often misuse it. I want to guide as many people as possible onto the right path.

Second, due to time constraints, I cannot coach everyone personally. So, this book is my gift to all plot owners, answering the question: *"How can you build an ultra-luxury house without a hefty budget, even without prior knowledge of construction?"*

I hope these lessons will steer you toward success and provide a fearless approach to developing your residential plot.

So, without further ado, let's explore *"How can you build an ultra-luxury house without a hefty budget, even without prior knowledge of construction?"*

Your friendly residential architect and Vastu expert,

Ar. Piyush Mittal

Chapter 1

SMILE! YOU ARE THE TRANSFORMATION!

Building your dream home is more than just a project—it's a journey of transformation. It's about creating a legacy, not just for yourself, but for your family and future generations. Before we dive into the nuts and bolts of construction, let's take a moment to celebrate YOU. Yes, YOU. The fact that you're here, reading this, means you've already taken the first step toward something extraordinary. You've acquired a piece of land, dreamed a dream, and decided to turn that dream into reality. That alone makes you a hero.

Let's pause for a moment. Think about it: in a world full of risks, challenges, and constant hustle, you've managed to secure a piece of this beautiful planet. You've shown courage, vision, and determination. You've dared to dream big—a dream that only a few have the guts to pursue. That's no small feat. You're not just building a house; you're crafting a sanctuary, a space that will nurture your family, inspire your loved ones, and stand as a testament to your hard work and vision.

You are a legacy maker. Every decision you make, every step you take, is shaping the future for your family and generations to come. You are setting an example, showing them what it means to take charge of your life and build something meaningful. YOU are a hero to your family.

But let's be honest—this journey isn't without its fears and challenges. The thought of overspending, delays, or things going wrong can be overwhelming. There will be challenges, no doubt. You might be asking yourself, "Can I really do this?" The answer is a resounding YES. You've already proven your ability to overcome obstacles by getting this far. Remember, every challenge has a solution, and every fear can be conquered and YOU have already proven that you have what it takes.

So, before we get into the technical details, I want you to do something for me. Smile. Yes, right now. Smile because you've already achieved something incredible. Smile because you're about to embark on one of the most rewarding journeys of your life. Smile because you're not just building a house—you're building a home, a legacy, and a future filled with love, laughter, and memories.

Remember This:

- **You are courageous:** You took the first step that many only dream of.
- **You are inspiring:** Your journey will motivate those around you.
- **You are in control:** Every challenge has a solution, and you will conquer them all.

This journey will have its ups and downs, but remember, you're not alone. With the right mindset, planning, and guidance, you'll navigate through it all with confidence. So, let's start this journey with a smile. You've earned it.

You are the transformation. You are the hero of this story. And this is just the beginning. Let's build something extraordinary—together.

Chapter 2

OVERCOMING THE BIGGEST FEARS IN HOME CONSTRUCTION

Building your dream home is exciting, but let's be honest—it can also be terrifying. It's a massive project, and it's natural to have fears. What if it goes over budget? What if there are delays? What if the final result doesn't match your vision? These fears are common, but the good news is that they can be managed and overcome. In this chapter, we'll address the biggest fears homeowners face during construction and how you can tackle them head-on.

Fear #1: "What If I Go Over Budget?"

One of the biggest fears homeowners have is the risk of overspending. Costs can spiral out of control if not planned properly, but with the right approach, you can stay within budget. Here's how:

- **Set a Realistic Budget**: Before starting, determine how much you're willing to spend, including a contingency fund for unexpected expenses.
- **Get Multiple Quotes**: Compare prices from different contractors and suppliers to ensure you're getting the best deal.

- **Prioritize Needs Over Wants**: Identify what's essential and what can wait. A luxury fixture may be tempting, but is it necessary?
- **Track Expenses Closely**: Keep a close eye on your spending to avoid surprises.

Fear #2: "What If I Hire the Wrong Contractor?"

A bad contractor can turn your dream into a nightmare. To avoid this:

- **Do Your Research**: Look for reputable builders with good reviews and previous successful projects.
- **Check Credentials**: Ensure they have the necessary licenses, certifications, and insurance.
- **Ask for References**: Speak to past clients about their experience.
- **Have a Clear Contract** : Everything should be in writing, from timelines to payment schedules, to avoid misunderstandings.

Fear #3: "What If the Project Takes Forever?"

Delays are common in construction, but they can be minimized:

- **Plan Ahead**: Finalize all design decisions before starting to prevent last-minute changes.
- **Work with Professionals**: An experienced architect and project manager can keep things on track.
- **Set a Timeline**: Ensure your contract includes a completion date with penalties for delays.
- **Stay Involved**: Regular site visits help keep everyone accountable and the project moving forward.

Fear #4: "What If My Home Doesn't Turn Out the Way I Imagined?"

It's frustrating to invest time and money only to end up with a result that doesn't meet your expectations. Avoid this by:

- **Creating a Clear Vision**: Look at pictures and plan exactly what you want.
- **Working with a Skilled Architect**: A good designer will translate your ideas into a functional and beautiful home.
- **Using 3D Renderings**: These allow you to see the design before construction begins, reducing surprises.
- **Communicating Clearly**: Frequent discussions with your contractor will ensure everyone is on the same page.

Fear #5: "What If There Are Hidden Issues?"

Unexpected problems like soil issues, plumbing complications, or electrical concerns can cause stress. Minimize risks by:

- **Conducting a Thorough Inspection**: Before starting, get a professional inspection of your land.
- **Choosing Quality Materials**: Cutting corners on materials can lead to costly repairs later.
- **Keeping a Contingency Fund**: Having a financial cushion ensures you're prepared for surprises.

Turning Fear Into Confidence

Every homeowner faces fears when building a home, but those who succeed are the ones who tackle them with knowledge and preparation. The key is to stay informed, work with the right people, and keep a positive mindset. Remember, this journey is about creating a space that reflects your vision and legacy.

So, take a deep breath. You are not alone in this process. By understanding your fears and proactively addressing them, you are already on the path to building your dream home with confidence. Let's move forward with excitement and clarity!

Chapter 3

THE RIGHT APPROACH: WHO TO TRUST & WHO TO IGNORE

The first three pieces of advice you receive can either make or break your project. Be extremely selective about whom you trust. There are numerous solutions to any problem—it's simply a matter of knowing the right way or asking the right question to get the right answer.

The first advice you take from three of your acquaintances shapes the entire scenario in your head, so it is of **ULTRA IMPORTANCE** to choose these three people wisely. The best advice on how to reach from point A to point B will always come from someone who has already traveled that path.

For example, I would never suggest taking advice from someone—no matter how close they are—who has only undergone a collaboration contract by selling a floor to a builder. They haven't walked the same path you are about to take. Seeking their advice could block your perspective and make you fearful of a problem that never existed in the first place.

A Real-Life Example

I still remember an incident from May 2019 when one of my cousins bought a new plot for his family. He wanted to build a soulful three-floor home, never planning to rent out or sell a floor. But after getting "advice" from his local property consultants (no offense), he nearly collapsed on the idea of a builder floor because, in their eyes, that was the only practical option.

His vision was almost hijacked by people with different priorities! Both he and his wife were shattered inside, as their dream was now sailing in a boat full of holes—holes of fear and anxiety. It was only after he called me for an insightful suggestion that he got realigned with his vision. Today, three years later, he is living happily in the home he always dreamed of.

Who Should You Trust?

- **An Architect with Expertise in Residential Homes:** Architects see the bigger picture. They ensure your home is not only beautiful but also functional and sustainable in the long term. Their expertise can turn your vision into reality while avoiding costly mistakes.
- **Homeowners Who Have Built a Similar Home Successfully:** There's no substitute for firsthand experience.
- **Experts Who Align with Your Vision, Not Just Trends:** Choose professionals who prioritize your goals over the latest trends. Your home should reflect your personality and needs, not just what's popular.

Who Should You Ignore?

- **Random Advice from Relatives & Neighbors Without Real Experience:** While well-meaning, their advice might not be based on practical knowledge or experience.
- **Contractors Giving Design Opinions:** Contractors are essential for execution, but they're not designers or planners. Rely on them for construction, not for design decisions.
- **Shortcuts That Sound Too Good to Be True:** If something sounds too good to be true, it probably is. Shortcuts often lead to costly mistakes and regrets.

GO GO GO GOVINDA!

Now, go out and set up meetings with the best consultants (architects) specializing in residential homes. The right consultant will enhance your property and envision it in ways you never imagined.

Did you ever notice that when you have an illness, you don't go directly to a medical shop? Instead, you consult a specialized doctor for expert advice. It's as simple as that.

Similarly, I highly recommend consulting an architect or designer before speaking with a contractor. Think of contractors as the medical shop—a step that comes after hiring the expert.

I am assuming that, given the powerful "YOU," you now have a consultant on board and are eager to know the IMMEDIATE NEXT STEP in the process.

So, let's not wait any longer—**move on to Chapter 4!**

Chapter 4

VASTU: THE SCIENCE OF ENERGY FLOW & HOW IT SHAPES YOUR HOME

When building your dream home, it's not just about the physical structure—it's also about creating a space that nurtures positive energy and harmony.

Why Vastu Matters

Vastu Shastra is a 5,000-year-old system that combines architecture, astronomy, and astrology to create balanced living spaces. It's based on the idea that every home is a living entity influenced by the five elements—earth, water, fire, air, and space. When these elements are in harmony, they create a positive energy flow, or prana, that enhances the well-being of the occupants.

The Importance of Precision in Vastu

Before diving into Vastu principles, it's crucial to get the orientation of your plot absolutely accurate. Using a mobile compass to determine directions is often unreliable because even a slight deviation of just 2 degrees out of 360° in the Vastu Purusha Mandala can disrupt the entire energy balance, making it impossible to achieve the desired results. Precision is non-negotiable in Vastu!

The BIGGEST Vastu Mistake: Entrance Direction Misconception

95% of plot owners believe that the front-facing side of their plot is the Vastu direction. But that's a major misconception!

Ask yourself this—do you sleep on the zero level (parking/stilt level)? No! That's where staff, house help, or drivers might stay. Your home's Vastu entrance is NOT the plot's entrance but the entrance of the built-up floor that YOU occupy, whether it's the upper ground floor, first floor, or beyond.

Vastu offers 32 possible entrance points, but only 11 are considered divine (daivik entrances)—choosing the right one is crucial for energy harmony.

The Right Service Core & Space Planning

After determining the ideal service core (which includes the staircase and lift lobby), focus on a spacious, well-thought-out layout. A great design isn't just about looks—it must enhance comfort, function, and flow.

Key Vastu Principles for Your Home

Here are some important guidelines to ensure positive energy in your home:

- **Main Entrance:** The entrance should be in the north, northeast, or east direction to allow good energy flow. Avoid having a door directly opposite a staircase.
- **Living Room:** This is the heart of your home. Place it in the northeast, north, or east direction to maintain peace and positivity.

- **Kitchen:** The southeast corner is ideal for the kitchen as it represents fire energy. Avoid placing it directly in front of the main entrance.
- **Bedrooms:** The master bedroom should be in the southwest direction for stability and peace. Avoid mirrors facing the bed, as they are believed to disturb sleep and cause stress.
- **Pooja Room:** The northeast corner is the best place for a pooja room or meditation space, ensuring spiritual well-being.
- **Bathrooms & Toilets:** They should be in the west or northwest direction to prevent negative energy from spreading.
- **Windows & Ventilation:** Proper airflow and sunlight are crucial. Ensure windows open to the east or north for good natural light and fresh air.

Practical Approach to Vastu

While Vastu is important, don't stress over every little detail. Modern homes may not allow 100% Vastu compliance, and that's okay! Focus on major aspects and create a home that feels comfortable, spacious, and filled with positive energy.

Your home should be a place of peace and happiness. Whether you believe in Vastu or not, applying these simple principles can help in designing a balanced and harmonious space. After all, a happy home leads to a happy life!

KNOW YOUR NEEDS/DESIRES: A Fun Yet Essential Exercise

Now, this fun yet powerful activity is something I do with every client during our first layout meeting. Every stakeholder—

even kids—gets a separate piece of paper to write down their deepest desires, needs, and must-haves for their new home.

This innocent sharing captures the purest essence of their vision and serves as the FIRST CANVAS for the masterpiece that follows.

Once these ideas are collected, sit together with your consultant to create a floor-wise plan—identifying which spaces and activities belong where and how they should connect.

Bringing It All Together: The Home of Your Dreams

This is the first time your family is openly sharing everything they want in their home. Now, take a fresh look—remove what's not needed, combine similar spaces, and make sure the layout feels open, practical, and comfortable.

Chapter 5

SANCTIONING AND CIVIL WORK INITIATIONS: HOW TO NAVIGATE THE APPROVAL PROCESS EASILY

Once your layout is carefully crafted to align with functionality and Vastu principles, the next critical step is getting your plans sanctioned and initiating civil work. This phase involves navigating approvals, selecting contractors, and ensuring a seamless start to construction. Here's a step-by-step guide to help you through this process without stress.

Step 1: Sanctioning the Plans

After finalizing the design, your consultant will prepare the necessary architectural and structural drawings. These plans need to be submitted to the local authority for approval. The sanctioning process can vary depending on your location, but your consultant will handle the paperwork and ensure compliance with local building codes.

Here is a Tip: While the plans are being sanctioned, ask your consultant to provide detailed structural drawings. This will allow you to initiate civil work as soon as the approvals are in place.

Step 2: Choosing the Right Contractors

During this phase, you'll need to engage civil contractors to begin construction. There are two types of civil contractors you can consider:

Labor Contractors: They provide only labor, and you supply the materials.

Material + Labor Contractors: They handle both labor and materials.

Key Considerations:

Hold a joint meeting with your consultant and contractor to finalize the scope of work, payment schedule, timelines, and timesheets.

Ensure all stakeholders are aligned from the start to avoid misunderstandings later.

The same process applies to selecting plumbing and electrical teams. These teams should be onboarded early so they're ready to begin work as soon as the civil work commences.

Step 3: Understanding Construction Timelines

In most cases, it takes around 50 days to cast the first slab, and each subsequent slab takes approximately 21 days in a single shuttering setup. Discuss these timelines thoroughly with your consultant and contractor to ensure the elevation design aligns with the slab casting schedule.

Remember: Quality construction depends on two critical factors—proper curing and high-quality materials. As the saying goes, "Jal hee jeevan hai" (Water is life). Proper curing with water is a must to ensure the strength and durability of the structure.

Step 4: Aligning Wet Works and Dry Works

As the brickwork progresses, it's essential to align the following teams to ensure a smooth workflow:

- **Electrical and HVAC Teams:** Pre-align these teams so they can complete their work before plastering begins.
- **Plastering Teams:** Once electrical and HVAC work is done, the plastering team can finish the walls.
- **Interior Design Teams:** Simultaneously, start discussions on interior design presentations, 3D renderings, and immersive virtual reality walkthroughs.

Here is a Tip: Prioritize quality waterproofing and plumbing to avoid future issues. Depending on weather conditions or your consultant's advice, you can proceed with either flooring or false ceiling work.

Step 5: Transitioning to Dry Works

Once all wet works (like plastering, waterproofing, marble laying, and POP) are near completion, you can move on to dry works such as:

- **Woodwork:** This includes cabinetry, doors, and furniture.
- **Painting and Finishing:** The final touches that bring your home to life.

Step 6: Stay Ahead with Planning

To avoid last-minute decision-making, align multiple meetings with your consultant to discuss upcoming tasks at least 2 months in advance. This proactive approach ensures you're never stuck making rushed decisions, which can be both daunting and intimidating.

Final Thoughts

Navigating the sanctioning and civil work phase can seem overwhelming, but with the right team and a clear plan, it becomes manageable. Your consultant is your pilot—they've guided many before you and will ensure you land safely.

Chapter 6

BUDGETING 2.0: THE SMART WAY TO CONTROL COSTS WITHOUT SACRIFICING LUXURY

Budgeting is often the most dreaded part of building a home. It can feel overwhelming, not just for homeowners but even for consultants. But what if I told you that budgeting doesn't have to be stressful? With the right approach, you can stay in control of your finances while still creating the home of your dreams. Let's break it down into simple, actionable steps.

Understanding the Two Types of Costs

To simplify budgeting, think of your expenses as two categories:

Fixed Costs (Type A) and **Variable Costs (Type B).**

Type A: Fixed Costs (Predetermined Expenses)

These are the costs that can be calculated and planned before the project begins. They include:

1. **Civil Structure (Till Plaster Stage):** The foundation, walls, and plastering.

2. **Plumbing and Electrical Conduiting:** The basic systems that run through your home.
3. **False Ceiling and Similar Materials:** Ceiling finishes and related components.
4. **Sanctioning and Out-of-Pocket Expenses:** Permits, approvals, and miscellaneous costs.
5. **Consultant's Fee:** Payments to your architect or designer.
6. **Labor Costs:** Approximate labor expenses for construction.
7. **Basic Furniture Costs:** Immovable and movable furniture.
8. **Lift and Electrical Appliances:** Costs for elevators and essential appliances.
9. **VRV/Air Conditioning:** HVAC systems for climate control.

These costs are relatively predictable and should be well-defined before starting the project. Work closely with your consultant to get accurate estimates and item rates from the market.

Type B: Variable Costs (Emotional or Unforeseen Expenses)

These are the costs that often spiral out of control if not monitored carefully. They include:

1. **General Market Inflation:** Rising prices of materials or labor during the project.
2. **Emotional Buying:** Decisions driven by emotions rather than practicality (very common when building a dream home).
3. **Premium Upgrades:** Choosing elite or high-end materials without proper justification.

4. **Lack of Material Comparison:** Not shopping around for the best prices.
5. **Wastage or Negligence:** Poor site management leading to material wastage.
6. **Improper Contracting:** Unclear contracts with contractors leading to unexpected costs.

The key to managing Type B costs is vigilance. Subtract your fixed costs (Type A) from your total budget, and the remaining amount is what you have for variable expenses. This balance is your buffer—keep a sharp eye on it to avoid overspending.

A Real-Life Example: Saving 27.5 Lakhs with Smart Choices

Let me share a personal story to illustrate the importance of monitoring Type B costs. During a project, my client and I decided to install an all-wooden ceiling (3000 sq. ft.) to create warmth on the main public floor of their duplex. The client, excited about the idea, sourced teak and pine wood planks costing Rs. 700/sq. ft., with additional expenses for polishing, ply, and frames, bringing the total to Rs. 1350/sq. ft.

However, I recognized this as a Type B cost. After careful analysis, I suggested an alternative: a flat POP ceiling (Rs. 100/sq. ft.) with commercial ply and a 1.2mm laminate to replicate the wooden look. The total cost came down to Rs. 430/sq. ft., saving the client Rs. 27.5 lakhs. The best part? No one could tell the difference because the ceiling was 11 feet high and untouchable.

This example highlights the importance of scrutinizing Type B costs. Emotional decisions can lead to unnecessary expenses, but with a sharp eye and practical alternatives, you can achieve the same results without breaking the bank.

Tips for Effective Budgeting

1. **Plan Ahead:** Define your fixed costs (Type A) before starting the project.
2. **Monitor Variable Costs:** Keep a close watch on Type B expenses and avoid emotional buying.
3. **Compare Materials:** Always shop around and explore cost-effective alternatives.
4. **Communicate with Your Consultant:** Regular meetings will help you stay on track and make informed decisions.
5. **Stay Disciplined:** Stick to your budget and resist the temptation to overspend.

Final Thoughts

Budgeting doesn't have to be overwhelming. By understanding the difference between fixed and variable costs, and staying vigilant about emotional spending, you can build your dream home without financial stress. Remember, affordable luxury is about making smart choices—not compromises.

With the right mindset and a clear plan, you can create a home that's both beautiful and budget-friendly.

Chapter 7

FINDING THE PERFECT ARCHITECT: THE KEY TO A STRESS-FREE BUILD

Choosing the right architect is like finding the perfect co-pilot for your home-building journey. This one decision can determine whether your project is a smooth flight or a bumpy ride. A skilled architect doesn't just create beautiful designs—they help you avoid costly mistakes, ensure functionality, and make the entire process stress-free.

Why the Right Architect Matters

An architect is more than just a designer; they're your guide, problem-solver, and advocate throughout the construction process. They ensure your home is functional, aesthetically pleasing, and compliant with local regulations. A great architect will:

- Translate your ideas into a practical design.
- Manage budgets and timelines effectively.
- Coordinate with contractors and other professionals.
- Anticipate challenges and provide solutions.

Qualities to Look for in an Architect

1. **Experience and Expertise:** Look for an architect with a strong portfolio of residential projects similar to your vision. Check their credentials, reviews, and past work.
2. **Communication Skills:** Your architect should listen to your needs, explain complex ideas clearly, and keep you informed at every stage.
3. **Attention to Detail:** A good architect pays attention to the smallest details, ensuring every aspect of your home is thoughtfully designed.
4. **Problem-Solving Ability:** Construction projects often face unexpected challenges. Your architect should be proactive in finding solutions.
5. **Alignment with Your Vision:** Choose someone who understands your style, preferences, and budget.

How to Find the Right Architect

1. **Research:** Start by searching online, asking for recommendations, or visiting local architecture firms.
2. **Interview:** Meet with potential architects to discuss your project. Ask about their experience, design philosophy, and approach to budgeting and timelines.
3. **Portfolio Review:** Examine their past projects to see if their style aligns with your vision.
4. **References:** Speak to their previous clients to understand their working style and reliability.

5. **Chemistry:** Trust your instincts. You'll be working closely with your architect, so it's essential to have a good rapport.

The Architect-Client Relationship

A successful project hinges on clear communication and mutual trust. Be open about your budget, expectations, and concerns. At the same time, trust your architect's expertise and be open to their suggestions.

Final Thoughts

Finding the perfect architect is the first step toward a stress-free build. Take your time, do your research, and choose someone who not only has the skills but also shares your vision. With the right architect by your side, your dream home will become a reality—smoothly, beautifully, and without unnecessary stress.

Chapter 8

FROM PLOT TO PLAN: WHAT YOU MUST FINALIZE BEFORE BREAKING GROUND

Before the first brick is laid, there's a lot of groundwork to be done. The period between acquiring your plot and starting construction is crucial. It's when you lay the foundation—not just for your home, but for the entire project's success. Here's a checklist of what you must finalize before breaking ground to ensure a smooth and stress-free build.

1. **Finalize Your Design and Layout:**

   Your home's design is the blueprint for everything that follows. Work closely with your architect to finalize the layout, ensuring it aligns with your lifestyle, needs, and Vastu principles (if applicable). Consider factors like room placement, natural light, ventilation, and future expansion.

2. **Obtain Necessary Approvals and Permits:**

   Before construction begins, ensure all necessary approvals and permits are in place. This includes building plans, environmental clearances, and utility connections. Your architect or consultant can guide you through this process, ensuring compliance with local regulations.

3. **Set a Realistic Budget and Timeline:**

   A clear budget and timeline are essential to keep the project on track. Break down costs into fixed and variable expenses (as discussed in Chapter 6) and allocate a contingency fund for unexpected costs. Similarly, establish a realistic timeline that accounts for potential delays.

4. **Choose the Right Contractor:**

   Your contractor will bring your design to life, so choose wisely. Look for someone with experience in similar projects, a good track record, and clear communication skills. Finalize the scope of work, payment schedule, and timelines in a written contract.

5. **Plan for Utilities and Services:**

   Ensure your plot has access to essential utilities like water, electricity, and sewage. If not, make arrangements for connections or alternative solutions. Also, plan for waste management and rainwater harvesting systems if required.

6. **Conduct a Site Analysis:**

   A thorough site analysis helps identify potential challenges like soil quality, drainage issues, or slope variations. This information is crucial for designing the foundation and ensuring the structural integrity of your home.

7. **Finalize Material Selection:**

   Decide on the materials you'll use for construction, finishes, and fixtures. This includes everything from bricks and cement to flooring and paint. Early selection helps avoid delays and ensures consistency in quality.

8. **Prepare for Construction Logistics:**

   Plan for storage of materials, temporary utilities, and site access for workers and equipment. Ensure safety measures are in place to protect workers and the site.

Final Thoughts

The pre-construction phase is your opportunity to set the stage for a successful build. It's where you turn your vision into an actionable plan. I remember working with a client who was so eager to start construction that they skipped some of these steps. The result? Delays, budget overruns, and a lot of stress. Don't let that be you.

Take your time, consult, and break ground only when you're fully prepared. Your dream home is worth the effort. Remember, a well-planned start leads to a well-built home. So, take a deep breath, trust the process, and get ready to build something extraordinary. Your dream home is just around the corner!

Chapter 9

SPATIAL PLANNING: HOW TO MAKE YOUR HOME FEEL BIGGER & MORE LUXURIOUS

Want your home to feel bigger and more luxurious? You don't need a huge space or a big budget. With some smart ideas, even a small home can feel open, comfortable, and fancy. Here's how you can do it:

1. **Keep It Open:**

   Instead of having too many walls, try combining spaces like the living room, dining area, and kitchen into one big open area. This makes your home feel larger and lets light flow freely. Use furniture like sofas or rugs to separate areas without closing them off.

2. **Let the Light In:**

   Light is a powerful tool in spatial planning. Large windows, skylights, and glass doors can flood your home with natural light, making it feel airy and open. Use sheer curtains or blinds to control light without blocking it. Mirrors strategically placed opposite windows can also amplify light and create the illusion of more space.

3. **Use Height Wisely:**

   Think upwards, not just sideways. High ceilings and tall windows draw the eye upward, creating a sense of grandeur. Use vertical storage solutions like floor-to-ceiling cabinets or shelves to free up floor space. Statement lighting fixtures like chandeliers or pendant lights can also emphasize height.

4. **Keep It Simple:**

   Too much stuff can make a home feel small and messy. Choose simple furniture with clean designs. Use items that do more than one job, like a stool that also works as storage. Keep decorations minimal—pick a few nice things instead of filling the space with too many items.

5. **Choose the Right Colors:**

   Light colors like white, cream, or light gray make a room feel bigger and more open. You can add a pop of color with cushions, artwork, or a single wall. Using the same color family for walls, furniture, and curtains can also make the space feel more connected and spacious.

6. **Smart Storage:**

   Clutter makes a home feel smaller. Use clever storage ideas like built-in cabinets, shelves under stairs, or hidden drawers. This keeps your home tidy and makes it look more luxurious.

7. **Add Fancy Touches:**

   Use good-quality materials like marble, wood, or polished tiles to make your home feel special. These materials not only look elegant but also stand the test of time. Pay attention to details like door handles, faucets, and light switches—small touches can make a big difference.

Final Thoughts

You don't need a big house to feel like you're living in luxury. By keeping things open, letting in light, using height, and keeping it simple, you can make any home feel bigger and more beautiful. Remember, it's not about the size of your home—it's about how you use the space. With these tips, you can create a home that's comfortable and inviting.

Chapter 10

Material Selection: The Hidden Industry Secrets to Save Money & Get Quality

Choosing the right materials for your home is like picking the ingredients for a recipe—get it right, and the result is amazing; get it wrong, and it can ruin everything. But here's the good news: you don't have to spend a fortune to get high-quality materials. With a few insider tips, you can save money without compromising on quality. Let's uncover some hidden industry secrets to help you make smart choices.

1. **Plan Ahead and Research:**

   Before you start shopping, know exactly what you need. Make a list of materials for each part of your home—floors, walls, ceilings, etc. Research online, visit stores, and compare prices. Don't rush; take your time to understand the options.

2. **Buy in Bulk:**
   Many suppliers offer discounts for bulk purchases. If you're buying materials like tiles, wood, or paint, ask about bulk rates. This can save you a lot of money, especially for larger projects.

3. **Local vs. Imported:**

   Imported materials often come with a high price tag. Instead, explore local options. Many local brands offer excellent quality at a fraction of the cost. Plus, local materials are often better suited to your climate and environment.

4. **Look for Alternatives:**

   You don't always need the most expensive option to get a luxurious look. For example, instead of natural marble, consider high-quality marble-look tiles. They're cheaper, easier to maintain, and look just as good. Similarly, laminate flooring can mimic the look of hardwood at a lower cost.

5. **Timing Matters:**

   Prices of materials can vary depending on the season. For example, grabbing Diwali offers on home appliances can save you nearly 30 percent. Keep an eye out for sales and promotions.

6. **Negotiate with Suppliers:**

   Don't be afraid to negotiate. Many suppliers are willing to offer discounts, especially if you're buying in large quantities or paying upfront. Building a good relationship with your supplier can also lead to better deals in the future.

7. **Quality Over Quantity:**

   While it's tempting to cut costs, don't compromise on quality for critical areas like plumbing, electrical, or structural materials. Cheap materials in these areas can lead to costly repairs later. Spend wisely on essentials and save on decorative items.

Final Thoughts

Material selection doesn't have to be a stressful or expensive process. With a little planning, research, and smart choices, you can get high-quality materials without breaking the bank. Remember, the goal is to create a beautiful, durable home that fits your budget. Use these insider tips to make informed decisions and enjoy the process of building your dream home.

Chapter 11

MUST-HAVE ELEMENTS FOR A MAINTENANCE-FREE HOME

Let's face it—nobody wants to spend their weekends fixing leaks, battling termites, or dealing with electrical issues. A maintenance-free home isn't just a dream; it's totally possible if you plan smartly. Here are five must-have elements to ensure your home stays beautiful and hassle-free for years to come.

1. **Termite Prevention – The Hidden Truth:**

   Okay, let's bust a myth first. Everyone thinks termites come from the soil, right? Well, here's a story that will change your mind.

   About 7 years ago, I was approached by a young couple who wanted me to design their penthouse on the 26th floor in Gurugram. I was pleasantly surprised when the young man (now a good friend) asked me a rather unexpected question:

   "Sir, I would love to get the penthouse designed by you, but I need a satisfactory answer to my question first – I am a distributor of BAYER termite chemicals, and even their team couldn't answer this: why is there a heavy termite infestation in this penthouse, despite it being on the 26th floor?"

   The truth? Termites don't just come from the soil. They can hitch a ride on untreated wood or furniture during construction. In this case, improper storage of cartons brought the termites in. So, the lesson is simple: termite prevention isn't just about soil treatment—it's about proper material handling and storage. Use termite-resistant materials and chemicals during construction to keep these pests away.

2. **Waterproofing Done Right:**
   Water leaks are a nightmare. But here's the thing: 85% of leaks happen due to poor waterproofing during the brickwork stage, not after completion. Yes, you read that right.

   Never underestimate the importance of waterproofing. Whether it's your roof, bathroom, or basement, invest in high-quality waterproofing during construction. It's a small cost now that saves you from big headaches later.

3. **Skirting & Brick Salts – Avoiding Structural Damage:**

   Skirting might seem like a small detail, but trust me, it's a game-changer. Skirting protects the base of your walls from moisture, dirt, and damage, extending their lifespan.

   And then there's brick salts—those white deposits on walls that weaken the structure over time. Use anti-salts treatments during construction to prevent this issue. It's a small step that makes a big difference.

4. **Glass Coatings for Durability:**

   Glass surfaces add elegance to your home, but they need care. Nano-coating treatments for glass prevent stains, scratches, and watermarks, keeping them shiny and new for years. It's a small investment that saves you the hassle of frequent cleaning and repairs.

5. **Lighting & Electrical Planning:**

    Here's a tip: Proper electrical planning is non-negotiable. Install extra conduits during construction to accommodate future needs, like additional lights or appliances. This saves 50% on modification costs later.

    Also, use high-quality switches, wires, and fixtures to avoid frequent repairs. Trust me, good electrical planning is worth every penny.

Final Thoughts

A maintenance-free home is all about smart planning and quality materials. By focusing on termite prevention, waterproofing, skirting, glass coatings, and electrical planning, you can save time, money, and stress in the long run.

Remember, the effort you put in during construction pays off for decades. Let's build a home that's as carefree as it is beautiful!

LET'S BUILD YOUR DREAM TOGETHER

Congratulations on reaching this point! You now have the insider knowledge to create an ultra-luxury home with confidence. Now, it's time to take the next step—and maybe sip some coffee while we're at it!

Want to discuss your home project personally with me? I invite you to join me for an exclusive 1-on-1 coffee meeting. Over a cup of coffee (or chai, if that's your thing), we'll dive deep into your vision, clear all your doubts, and create a roadmap to turn your dream home into reality.

Schedule Your Meeting: +91 9711500133

Let's brew something extraordinary—together.

Your Friendly Residential Architect and Vastu Expert,

Ar. Piyush Mittal